• CONTENTS • CONTENTS • CONTENTS •

INTRODUCTION

Families – who needs them?

All children need a family – they provide you with a home, food, clothes, and they teach you how to live_as a member of society, and look after yourself as an adult.

Deep down we usually love our families and would do anything for them, but at some times in our lives (especially during our teenage years) we may find ourselves asking why we have to be stuck with such an annoying bunch of people!
But first let's think about what a family actually is. You may live with both your parents in a traditional **nuclear family** or you may only live with one parent. You may be adopted, **fostered** or living with grandparents, stepparents and step**siblings**. Families are not just the people you live with – they are the people you love, who take care of you and with whom you are bonded to within a family network. In the past, couples usually married before having children and stayed together no matter what.

'My family is the best.'

Now women have more financial independence and couples face less social pressure to stay in unhappy relationships. For the children that have to cope with a break-up or major upset in the family, it can be tough. Every family has issues – even the traditional nuclear family. In some families, parents are tougher on the eldest children, who in turn get their own back on their siblings.

COMMUNITY... TH

BY KA... S

Raintree

www.raintreepublishers.co.uk
Visit our website to find out more information about **Raintree** books.

To order:
☎ Phone 44 (0) 1865 888113
▤ Send a fax to 44 (0) 1865 314091
▢ Visit the Raintree bookshop at **www.raintreepublishers.co.uk** to browse our
catalogue and order online.

First published in Great Britain by Raintree,
Halley Court, Jordan Hill, Oxford OX2 8EJ,
part of Harcourt Education.
Raintree is a registered trademark of Harcourt
Education Ltd.

Raintree Editor: Kate Buckingham
Written by Kate Tym and Penny Worms
Packaged by ticktock Media Ltd.

With thanks to our expert advisers for their contributions
and all the young people who gave us their stories.

Printed and bound in China by South China
Printing Company.

ISBN 1 844 43408 7 (Hardback)
08 07 06 05 04
10 9 8 7 6 5 4 3 2 1

ISBN 1 844 43413 3 (Paperback)
09 08 07 06 05
10 9 8 7 6 5 4 3 2 1

British Library Cataloguing in Publication Data
Tym, Kate and Worms, Penny
Coping with Families
306.8'5
A full catalogue record for this book is available
from the British Library.

Acknowledgements
The publishers would like to thank the following for
permission to reproduce photographs: Alamy: OFC,
pp. **4** top left, **4–5** centre, **12–13** centre, **15** top,
16 top, **28–29** centre, **34** centre left, **40–41** centre,
41 bottom, **42** top. Comstock: OBC, pp. **10** top,
11, **13** top, **20** top, **21** centre, **22–23** centre, **26** top,
29 bottom. Digital Vision: **34–35**. PhotoAlto: pp. **6** top,
6–7 centre, **17**, **31** top, **32** top, **37** top. Roddy Payne
Photographic Studio: pp. **1**, **5** bottom right, **6** bottom,
7 top, **8** top, **9** top, **14** top, **18–19** centre, **18** top,
19 top, **23** top, **24** top, **25** top, **27**, **30** top, **33**, **35**
right, **36** top, **38** top, **39** bottom, **41** top right, **43**.

Every effort has been made to contact copyright holders
of any material reproduced in this book. Any omissions
will be rectified in subsequent printings if notice is given
to the publishers.

All Internet addresses (URLs) given in this book were
valid at the time of going to press. However, due to the
dynamic nature of the Internet, some addresses may
have changed, or sites may have changed or ceased to
exist since publication. While the author and publishers
regret any inconvenience this may cause readers, no
responsibility for any such changes can be accepted
by either the author or the publishers.

Or, for youngest children, parents can be putty in their hands, which can lead to **resentment** and anger in older siblings. And as for being stuck in the middle ... well maybe you get overlooked a little too often. Then there are issues with having no siblings, or too many, or ones that are forced upon you – can it get much more complicated? Well ... yes. You have to deal with parents not letting you do what you want to do; siblings invading your space and privacy; and sometimes even tragedy.

'I worry that my parents will split up.'

It's a wonder anyone ever survives having a family at all! So if you're tearing your hair out over problems with your family, this book can help. It takes a close look at different aspects of family life – how to deal with picky parents, annoying siblings or new stepparents. And when something sad or bad happens such as a family break-up, violence within a family, or the death of a family member, this book shows you how to cope. With true-life experiences and top tips, it's not only full of useful information, but it may help you realize that, whatever the issue, you're probably not alone and ... there's always a way to sort it out.

OUR EXPERT PANEL
THE EXPERTS GIVING ADVICE ARE ...

Anita Jardine
Parent of two teenagers and experienced family practitioner. Currently employed as a school counsellor for the NSPCC and involved in providing a solution-focused service for young people and their parents/carers.

Simon Howell
Simon Howell is a social worker and family therapist. He works for the NSPCC.

Mac Buckley
Mac Buckley is a family liaison officer. She has worked in residential homes, schools and family centres for children and young people.

CASE STUDIES
Within each chapter are case studies – true stories about real people who have had some kind of problem to overcome. Read their stories, check out the experts' advice and learn what actually happened in the end. All the names of the contributors have been changed to protect their identity and models have been used for the photographs.

PICKY PARENTS

COPING WITH UPTIGHT PARENTS

Even the most easy-going parents can get uptight at times – and when they do they can make your life a living hell!

Most parents want the best for their children. But even though they try their best, nobody ever taught them how to be parents so sometimes they can get it wrong.

Parenting teenagers can be particularly tricky for them. They know they've got to let go of you sooner or later, but they may feel reluctant to loosen the reins a minute too soon. Also, they're suddenly up against someone with the wit and arguing power to take them on at their own game. And the stakes are higher too. It's no longer just a case of arguing over putting your building bricks away, it's about bigger things: schoolwork, going out, attitude and independence. And then there are the potentially harmful life choices, such as smoking, piercings and drinking ... just what are Mum and Dad supposed to do about those?

The thing with parents is that they usually make decisions based on keeping you safe, using their knowledge and life experiences. They've seen lots of things in their time on the planet and they know about the worst-case scenarios.

'I can't talk to my dad. It always ends up in an argument.'

WHAT PARENTS WANT FROM YOU

To get what you want from your parents you need to think about giving them what they want in return. But just what do parents want?

- **To be appreciated**
- **To know they have brought you up well**
- **To trust you**
- **To know you are sensible about your own health and safety**
- **Your respect**
- **Your love**

Not only that, they have an idea of the kind of person they want you to be – whether it's polite, successful, open-minded or whatever – and so this sometimes clashes with how you really are or what you want. You need to feel **empowered** to make your own choices. Your parents need to make sure they are the right choices for your future.

Sometimes your parents' **expectations** of you can make you uncomfortable or unhappy. If they expect too much, the pressure can seem overwhelming. If they expect too little, you may give up, seeing little point in trying your best. So what do you do when you are at odds with your parents? However difficult or stubborn your parents are being, the way to get around them can actually be very straightforward. The trick is communication and **compromise** – in other words, talking to them and being prepared to meet them halfway. Show how mature and responsible you are and they should start to trust you. Show them you are sensible and savvy and it should give them the confidence to give you more freedom. Believe it or not, it's a much more effective method than silence or outright rebellion.

'I don't have a problem with my parents. I guess they trust me.'

7 TIPS FOR TALKING TO YOUR PARENTS

1 STAY CALM AND USE CHARM
Don't argue or shout – your parents are far more likely to listen to your point of view if you're not yelling.

2 SHOW YOUR PARENTS HOW MATURE YOU CAN BE
Showing them respect and appreciation will allow them to see how mature you can be and what a great job they've done bringing you up!

3 BE PREPARED TO COMPROMISE
It is unlikely that you will always agree with your parents. Whenever your opinions differ, try to compromise by meeting halfway.

4 KEEP FOCUSED
Don't waste your time discussing trivial or unrelated things. Keep focused on what you want to discuss.

5 TRY TO SEE THEIR POINT OF VIEW
You are more likely to get parents to co-operate if you show them you understand their point of view. That's so much more reasonable than shouting, 'You never let me do anything!'

6 ACT RESPONSIBLY
Trust is an important aspect of your relationship with your parents. If you make an agreement, then stick to it!

7 DON'T PUSH YOUR LUCK
If you reach a reasonable compromise, don't start all over again and try to get more out of them. It could backfire, leaving you with nothing.

CASE STUDY 1

I'M GROUNDED!

Cally, 14, went against her parents' wishes by getting her ear pierced and now she's suffering the consequences.

'My parents had never given me a reason why they didn't want me to get it done. It was just a hang-up.'

I asked my parents if I could get the top of my ear pierced and they said no. But when I went to a music festival with all my mates, I just thought, 'What's the harm?'

I mean, it's only one ear and they could always ask me to take it out. They had never given me a reason why they didn't want me to get it done. It was just a hang-up. Anyway, my hair's quite short so a lot of the time around my parents I took my earring out. I got away with it for three whole months. Then we were having dinner one evening and I tucked my hair behind my ear, totally forgetting that my earring was in. It was only a tiny red gem, really tiny, but my mum noticed and went absolutely psycho. Both she and Dad were so annoyed – they went completely over the top, saying I now wouldn't be allowed to go on this family trip to New York because I'd gone against their wishes. They put me through this total guilt-trip and I was really distraught about the trip. It's a tiny little bead in the top of my ear. It's not as if I've had 'Drop dead' tattooed on my forehead!

ASK THE EXPERTS...

Simon the social worker says...
The ability to face up to conflict is a useful life skill. However, there might be times when you would rather avoid it. If there is something you really want, tell your parents, explain how much it means to you and ask them to help you understand their point of view. You may not get what you want this time but you will have handled it the right way and they will remember it next time.

Anita the counsellor says...
Piercings can provoke very strong reactions in older people. Also, your piercing, however tiny, is one of the first signs to your parents that you are beginning to make individual choices they may not like. You need to accept that the process of them letting you have control over your life is a gradual one and it will be achieved one step at a time.

Mac the family liaison officer says...
It can be difficult to come to a compromise when your parents are strongly opposed to what you want. Next time a situation like this arises, you could try bringing the issue up when you are all sitting down to dinner – where there is no option but to have a discussion about it. Try to put your views forward in a respectful way and give your parents the chance to respond with their feelings.

MY DAD'S SO STRICT

Shani, 13, has a father who thinks she's too young to go on dates. When he discovers that she's been out with a boy, he takes her phone and says she can't be trusted to go into town with her friends again.

My dad's really traditional and strict. He doesn't let my sister and I go out during the week, and if we go out on Fridays, we have to tell him what we're doing.

He says things like, 'There had better not be any boys there'! Well, I was asked out by this boy and I really wanted to go. I said I was meeting my friend Sarah, so Dad dropped me off in town

'My mum says he's just protective. She pretends to go along with him.'

and I met this boy inside the shopping centre so Dad couldn't see. When I got home he sent me a text message saying would I like to go out again. I don't know how but my dad knew it was from a boy. He took my phone and read the message. He then went mad, saying I couldn't be trusted and that I wasn't going to be allowed to go into town on my own again. My mum says he's just protective. If he doesn't let me do what I want, I'll just have to carry on lying. It'll be his loss, because he won't know what I'm up to.

ASK THE EXPERTS...

Simon the social worker says...
When you're mature enough to go out with boys, you're old enough to sit down and talk to your father about **sex and relationships!** Introduce the subject by asking him how he met his first girlfriend. Talk to him about how he started dating. Then help him see that boys are already a part of your life and you can't just avoid them. Get his support and advice on dating boys safely.

Anita the counsellor says...
It sounds as if your dad cares a lot about you and your sister. He wants to keep you safe but this can be **really hard on you when other friends have more freedom.** You're lucky to have an understanding mum and she may be able to help you talk to your dad to reassure him. Being truthful is more likely to build up trust between you in the long run.

Mac the family liaison officer says...
It can be difficult for your parents when you start **dating.** They might be a bit out of touch! It sounds as though you really need to sit down and have a heart-to-heart with your parents. Think of this as your chance to show them how mature you can be. Together, you might be able to make some ground rules that you are both happy with.

MY MUM'S A CONTROL FREAK

Archie, 15, is losing respect for his mum because she is overly critical of him and tries to control everything he does.

My mum is a control-freak.

It's, 'You're not going there, it's really rough ... I don't know who you're going with ... there could be drugs ... you've got school tomorrow...' If I do get to go anywhere, I get a really early curfew. If I break it, I'm grounded for a week. One day I wanted to go to this really cool party. I went to my mate's in the afternoon without telling Mum and then went to the party. I stayed at my mate's that night. When I went home Mum went **ballistic,** saying I was grounded for life. She decided she had to drop me off and pick me up from school but there was NO WAY I was going to be humiliated in front of my friends, so I just didn't turn up for the lifts. She goes on about me to my Gran as if I am this totally out-of-control kid, but I've never done anything bad. I just want a bit of a life.

> 'The older I get the worse it is.'

ASK THE EXPERTS...

Simon the social worker says...
Having a good reputation is important to everyone. The question is can you have a good reputation at home with your family and at school with your mates? The answer is that you can but it means working at it. Take the lead and talk to your mum. Tell her what you want and listen to her point of view. Stop waiting for her to tell you what to do and show her you can cope.

Anita the counsellor says...
You have insight into the fact your mum is very controlling and prone to worry about you when there's no need. Hopefully you can use this understanding to put your point of view across to her. You need to try and negotiate more freedom, which could be more effective than rebelling. Let her know that it's hurtful to be accused when you can be trusted to make sensible choices over issues such as drugs.

Mac the family liaison officer says...
Although rebelling might seem to solve the problem in the short term, it's only going to make your mum trust you less. Try sitting down and talking things through. If you still feel as though you can't get through to her, try getting a relative or family friend to understand your frustration and speak to her on your behalf.

THE OUTCOMES

After reading our experts' advice, Cally, Shani and Archie wrote back to let us know how things turned out...

C A S E   S T U D Y   1

Give it time

I had to promise never to do anything like that again – well, until I'm 16 anyway! They were angry for days, but then my mum said what's done is done and she just got over it. Dad was really rude about the earring, saying it looked awful and being generally bad-tempered, but I still love it and don't regret having it done at all. I suppose I regret not getting Mum's permission first – it probably wouldn't have been that hard to persuade her, and she might have even bought me new earrings. She refuses now – on principle (whatever that means!)

GET CONNECTED

FOLLOW THIS WEB LINK TO FIND OUT MORE:

www.kidzworld.com

An American magazine-style website with games, news, entertainment and gossip. There's plenty of advice and you can write in with your own parent problem.

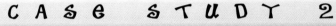

C A S E   S T U D Y   2

Find a way around it

I still have to lie to Dad but I do tell Mum where I'm going. She keeps it to herself because she understands that I want to go out and she'd rather know where I'm going than be lied to. In a way my mum's lying too, but she knows how my dad will react.

You just can't talk to him. I know he's just being protective because he cares, but he tried to control my older sister's life and now she's left home. I don't want him doing the same to me. Thank goodness my mum's more reasonable or it would be a nightmare.

C A S E   S T U D Y   3

Communicate and compromise

The final straw was when I found Mum going through my drawers. She said she needed to do it because I wouldn't communicate with her. I just completely lost it. When I'd run out of steam, we started talking, calmly. It all came out and she just took it. She agreed that it was hard for her not to butt in and take over. We then started to negotiate. She said I could go to the skate-park if I promised to keep my weekday curfew. I agreed if I could have a later curfew at weekends and go to parties. Ever since then, we're getting on okay.

REMEMBER
- Parents usually have your best interests at heart.
- Communication and compromise are the key.
- Negotiate to get what you want.
- Find ways to gain their trust.
- TALK – don't hide your feelings or suffer in silence.

THE FACTS

- Divorce is when a marriage is legally ended by the courts. After a divorce, your parents are no longer husband and wife.

- Separation is when your parents live apart. They can get a legal separation, or it can be an informal agreement between them.

- Around 150,000 children in the UK go through a divorce every year.

- About 650 children see their parents separate or get divorced every day.

- The most common reasons for divorce:

  - They've grown apart
  - They want different things
  - One or both want to be with someone else
  - Constant rows or disagreements
  - They don't spend enough time together

PARENTAL PARTING

FROM SHORT SPLIT TO DREADED DIVORCE

About one in every four children have parents who divorce. The rest often worry about it.

The words 'We're splitting up' are some that most children dread ever hearing.
It's not only the parting that has an effect on you – often the build-up to separation or divorce can be almost as bad as the divorce itself. In the very best circumstances, parents can stay civil to each other – or even remain friends. After a while, you may even agree that it's a good thing – the rows stop, your parents are happier and you have two homes instead of one. A break-up at its worst can see your parents at each other's throats and you could be caught in the crossfire.

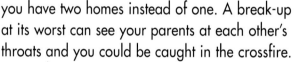

'I realize now that they are happier apart.'

The most important thing to remember if your parents do part is that it's not happening because of you. They have fallen out of love with each other, not with you, and none of it is your fault. Equally, nothing you say or do will heal their relationship.

'I just want them to get back together.'

What you can do though is make it easier for yourself and your **siblings**. Ask the questions you want answers to. If Dad is pumping you for information about Mum, tell him you won't discuss either of them with the other. If Mum is making you feel guilty about loving and wanting to see Dad, you need to tell her that you just want to be allowed to love them both. Divorce is not always a mutual decision, and one of your parents may find it devastating. You can try to help them through the difficult times, but you, too, need support. Support from a sibling or grandparent can be ideal, but friends can also help, especially if they've been through a similar thing. And then there are the professionals – you could talk to a teacher, counsellor or helpline (see p. 47). Give it time. The divorce process usually takes more than six months, but over that time it will get increasingly better for all of you as you adjust to the change.

HOW TO DEAL WITH...

When your parents are going through a divorce, they can be emotional and even irrational. Here's how to deal with some common situations:

1 THEY ARE USING YOU TO GET INFORMATION ABOUT EACH OTHER
The most sensible way to handle this is to avoid talking to each parent about the other.

2 THEY ARGUE WHEN THEY MEET
Talk to them individually so they realize how much their arguing upsets you.

3 ONE PARENT IS MORE UPSET
This is often a consequence of divorce and separation. There may be more to it than you know and they're probably dealing with it in different ways.

4 THEY ARE MORE DEPENDENT ON YOU
Lone parents can rely more on their children for companionship and help than two-parent families. Support your parent at this difficult time, but don't forget to balance it with living your own life.

5 THEY'RE ACTING LIKE TEENAGERS
A new sense of freedom can sometimes have a strange effect on separated parents. They may start dressing and acting differently, which could be an embarrassment for you! Just remember, it's probably a passing phase – they are likely to turn back into your good old reliable parent soon.

13

THEY'RE BETTER OFF APART

Adam, 15, has come to terms with his parents' divorce but now he suspects the reason was Dad's new girlfriend.

'After everything had calmed down, they were that much happier. They were even able to be civil to each other around us.'

When my parents finally split up, it was actually a bit of a relief. I think they'd been trying to hold things together for years.

They were always arguing and bitching at each other. Dad was drinking too much and Mum had started smoking just to get to him. It was mad! So when they finally split up, it was really terrible, but after everything had calmed down they were that much happier. They were even able to be civil to each other around us, which they hadn't bothered about for years.

Dad's getting remarried in the autumn. No one's said anything, but I'm pretty sure the woman, Meg, was having an affair with him for years before. So I guess she'll be happy now she's finally managed to get him. Mum won't talk about it. She says, 'I won't be able to say anything nice, so I won't say anything at all!', which makes me laugh because she might as well be saying, 'I totally hate that woman!' Meg's okay though. And Dad's happy.

ASK THE EXPERTS...

Simon the social worker says...
Weddings aren't always the happy occasions they're cracked up to be. If an affair brought the newly-weds together they can be humiliating occasions for the person who was dumped. Be **sensitive** to your mum's feelings – thankful she's not saying what she really thinks – and help stop old wounds opening up too much by not talking about Meg or the wedding plans around your mum.

Anita the counsellor says...
It's hard to be in a situation with divided loyalties but you seem to have been able to get through the hard times and to be **philosophical** about **things.** This maturity will help you adapt to whatever changes come up following your dad's remarriage as the adults begin to reorganize their lives.

Mac the family liaison officer says...
There's no easy way through a parental break-up. But it sounds like you've managed to keep your head so far. It's understandable that your mum might feel a bit angry or wronged by the situation – and it's to her credit that she isn't discussing these feelings with you so that you feel caught in the middle. Remember – change can be tough at the time but can open doors to new, positive experiences if you're open to them.

I CAN'T BELIEVE THEY'VE SPLIT UP

'I cry all the time and ask my mum why they can't get back together.'

Ellen, 13, is still having a hard time accepting the break-up of her parents last year.

My mum and dad split up last year and I still just can't believe it. I cry all the time and ask my mum why they can't get back together.

I know it gets on her nerves, because she tells me to leave it alone. She says, 'Ellen, we just can't, okay!'

My dad's moved about 450 kilometres away so I hardly see him. He phones all the time but it's not the same and I feel weird about going to visit him somewhere that's not home, but his job moved and I think Mum decided she didn't want to go with him. I wouldn't want to change schools or leave my friends, but I would if it meant them getting back together.

ASK THE EXPERTS...

Simon the social worker says...
The reality is that your parents have gone their separate ways and you're left with two people who are heading **in opposite directions.** You can't pull them back together and you can't keep up with them both at the same time. Recharge your batteries by doing fun things with friends. And give yourself plenty of time to get used to the way things are now.

Anita the counsellor says...
What a difficult time you've had – losing your dad from your day-to-day life and not being able to talk to your **mum about it.** Is there anyone else in the family or at school that you could talk to about how down you're feeling? Friends may have had a similar experience. Sharing your worries with friends or others you can talk to will help you keep yourself together through this.

Mac the family liaison officer says...
It might seem impossible to imagine adjusting to these new circumstances. You will feel better about things in time. If you can't talk to your mum, try confiding in a school counsellor or a friend. The first step to feeling better is getting all your feelings off your chest. Then, when you're feeling a bit stronger, you can plan holidays to visit your dad. Even though the living arrangements have changed, your parents still love you.

15

MY MUM'S SO NASTY

Thomas, 13, is feeling angry with his mum. He blames her for splitting up the family and driving his dad away.

I knew something was up. I heard Dad on the phone saying he was leaving before Mum told me.

He had his bags packed one morning when I came down the stairs and said he was moving out and he would call me. He said it would all be okay, but he looked like he was going to cry. That choked me up. I've never seen my dad about to cry before. As soon as he was out the door, Mum started shoving everything of his into bags. Pictures we'd had on our wall for ages of Dad and me at football and stuff, all got shoved in a bag and put in the garage. Like she wants him gone. Now when he calls, she's really horrible to him and gets really stressed with me if I want to see him. She won't let him in the house when he comes to visit and is always saying bad things about him. She split up our family – she drove him away and I have to live with her because Dad's in some crummy bedsit.

> 'When he calls, she's really horrible to him and gets really stressed with me if I want to see him.'

ASK THE EXPERTS...

Simon the social worker says...
A lot of families get into playing the blame game. Blaming others for our problems can be very satisfying. The trouble is that we can end up losing people if we take sides. So support your dad and don't take it out on your mum because she's probably hurt too. Most of all, though, don't forget your own needs in the situation. Remind your parents that you have feelings too and get them to focus on you again.

Anita the counsellor says...
It's not easy when parents aren't able to be adult in a situation and it sounds like your mum is struggling with this. She's clearly been hurt by your dad. Try telling her how you feel when she puts him down or lays a guilt trip on you about seeing him. If this isn't helpful, is there anyone who could talk to her for you about your need to see your dad – another family member, perhaps?

Mac the family liaison officer says...
When a relationship breaks down, it's easy to point the finger at someone – but the reality is, it's rarely one person's fault. Whatever the trigger for your parent's break-up, one or both of them must have been pretty unhappy for it to come to this. No one's perfect – your mum and dad are going to have different ways of dealing with this. Be patient with your mum – she'll eventually work her negative feelings out.

THE OUTCOMES

After reading our experts' advice, Adam, Ellen and Thomas wrote back to let us know how things turned out...

CASE STUDY 1

It's all worked out

Ultimately, I wish we could have been the kind of happy family that stays together for ever, but we weren't. Well, they weren't so we're all better off if they're apart. Dad got remarried. We're getting used to Meg and like going round there. I don't stay because I like to be in my own bed, which annoys my dad a bit, but my sister stays and she and Meg get on well. Mum's going out a lot – I'm glad because I want her to have someone so she's not on her own when my sister and I leave home.

CASE STUDY 2

It does get better

Dad still calls a lot but I haven't seen him for ages. Mum never talks about him. She's got a boyfriend now and that makes me miss Dad even more. Dad asked me to go up in the summer holidays and when I asked Mum she got all annoyed about it, but she agreed, if Dad came down to get me. I'm really looking forward to it. I still really wish that Mum and Dad would get back together, but I suppose that will never happen now she's got this bloke.

CASE STUDY 3

Get help

Dad's buying a house and I want to go and live with him, but I've got to tell my mum and I know she'll be really upset. She makes me feel so guilty about seeing Dad, but Dad's not like that about Mum. His house is not far from Mum's, so I'll still see her all the time – the difference is that Dad will be completely cool about it. Dad says what I want is the most important thing, and it *is* what I want. I've decided to ask my gran to help. Hopefully, she can help me talk to Mum. I don't want to hurt Mum anymore, but my feelings are important too.

REMEMBER

• Parents split up because they fall out of love with each other, but they still love you.
• You are not alone – 650 children in the UK go through the same thing every day.
• Talk about your worries and your feelings. It really helps.
• Things do get easier over time.

GET CONNECTED

FOLLOW THESE WEB LINKS TO FIND OUT MORE:

www.youthinformation.com

An excellent site offering information about the legal aspects of divorce.

www.parentlineplus.org.uk

The children and young people's section of this site tells you what to expect when your parents divorce.

www.childline.org.uk

The website of the national young people's helpline, offering advice and counselling.

See p. 47 for other useful contacts and helplines

17

BEREAVEMENT

COPING WITH a DEATH IN THE FAMILY

HELPING A FRIEND

If a friend has lost someone close to them, here are some ways you can help...

- **Tell them how sorry you are**
  Don't ignore what has happened or avoid them. It will make them feel worse.

- **Don't be frightened to talk to them about it**
  If they don't want to talk they will tell you. It doesn't mean they don't ever want to talk about it.

- **Let them know you are there for them**
  Whether they want to talk, shout, cry or just be distracted for a while.

- **Don't be pushed away**
  Your friend may withdraw for a while. Give them the space they need, but reassure them that you'll always be their friend. Don't stop inviting them to places – they may turn you down for months, but there will come a time when they are ready to be sociable again.

The death of someone you love can turn your world upside-down and is one of the most difficult experiences to endure.

Grief is not just one feeling but a whole *succession* of different feelings – all of which take time to work through. There is no right or wrong way to behave in such a situation.

The mixture of emotions can make you feel confused or worried that you're not reacting 'normally', but there's no textbook guide to how you'll feel or how you should behave. The death of a family member means that your family is not the same anymore, and never will be. It may make you think how **vulnerable** everyone is and start to worry about your own and other peoples' **mortality**. There may be some guilt over how you behaved or thought about the person who has died.

'I wanted to fight it, but everyone else was resigned to the fact that he was going to die.'

Family and friends can help and a **sympathetic** arm around the shoulders or a comforting hug can express love in a way words cannot. But, ultimately, grief is something you go through in a very personal way. The experts' view is that talking about your feelings is a better way of dealing with death than bottling it all up inside. Don't be afraid to show your emotions. If another family member is preventing you from doing this because they are dealing with their own grief in a different way, then you need to find others who will listen. You need to be allowed to express your grief as it is all part of the healing process. The comforting news is that eventually the intensity of your grief will subside. As time passes, the raw pain will become less overwhelming – and although there will always be reminders of what has happened and the pain you felt, there will also come a point where you can hold on to the nice memories and take comfort from the time you did have with that special person.

HOW LONG DOES IT TAKE?

The closer the person was to you, the longer it will take. It really depends on the bond you had with the person. It can also depend on the cause of death. **Grieving** cannot be rushed. It will take as long as it takes for you to feel back to your normal self again. It might happen in short bursts to start with, but it will happen.

'It was hard to talk to people.'

10 FEELINGS YOU MAY HAVE

If a family member dies, you may go through a huge range of emotions. Here are some common feelings:

1 SADNESS
You may not feel like crying, it doesn't mean you're not sad.

2 GUILT
You may want to turn back the clock to change something you did or said.

3 DISBELIEF
It can take a while for the death to sink in.

4 ABANDONED
You may feel lonely or left behind.

5 ANGER
Find a safe outlet for these feelings, such as a pillow or a punch bag.

6 CONFUSION
Things that made sense before the death might not make sense now.

7 ANXIETY
You may fear for the rest of your family.

8 NUMB
An overdose of feelings can make you numb.

9 DESPAIR
You may feel that everything is pointless.

10 BELIEF
If things have been difficult or upsetting prior to their death.

19

THE WORST DAY OF MY LIFE

Joe, 15, watched his father getting more and more ill from cancer two years ago. Then he had to cope with his death.

My dad died two years ago of cancer. It was the worst thing that ever happened to me.

We had to go and visit him in the hospital towards the end, and I just didn't want to go. He just didn't look like my dad anymore. I kept asking, 'They're going to find a way to make him better, aren't they?' But everyone else seemed resigned to it. I couldn't believe that my mum would just roll over and accept that he was going to die. And then when he did die, it was a weird void. I couldn't believe I

'It was like my whole life had exploded.'

would never see him again. My mum went on auto-pilot for a year. She used to be a really good cook and make nice meals but after Dad died, she obviously couldn't be bothered – everything came out of a packet! She tried to stay positive in front of us but I knew she wasn't all right. And I know she didn't sleep, because I'd hear her getting up in the night. My sister just went really quiet. I felt like I wanted to talk about Dad but everyone just got too upset, so I just left it.

ASK THE EXPERTS...

Simon the social worker says...
Everyone has their own way of dealing with death. When a family member dies it's not unusual for the people who are left behind to retreat inside themselves to lick their wounds. Over time they do gradually come out of themselves again. Talking to friends and family can help it happen. And when a family is ready to come together again, they can share happier memories and remember the person they lost.

Anita the counsellor says...
You've had to come to terms with the changes your dad went through when he was ill as well as losing him to the cancer. This is a massive thing for anyone to cope with. Maybe you can start to talk to other family members and share memories of how your dad was when he was well. There is an organization called Cruse which could help you do this if you feel stuck as a family. (See pp. 21 and 47 for contact details.)

Mac the family liaison officer says...
You cannot put a time limit on the healing period following a death in the family. It differs for everyone – as do people's methods for coping with the loss. If your family can't deal with talking about your dad, try a school counsellor or perhaps a member of your extended family. Make sure your family know when they do want to talk about your dad, that you are there for them too.

THE OUTCOME

Joe told us how things turned out...

CASE STUDY 1

Do something positive

It's starting to get a bit better now. If I say, 'Do you remember when Dad did something funny...', we're all able to talk and laugh about it. I like that more than not talking about him. I don't want to forget him. I look at pictures of when we were on holiday, when he was well, and I try to remember him that way. I do get choked up but I try to keep a lid on it. My mates don't want me blubbing all the time — they wouldn't know how to handle it.

GET CONNECTED

FOLLOW THESE WEB LINKS TO FIND OUT MORE:

www.crusebereavementcare.org.uk

A website for anyone affected by the death of a loved one.

www.winstonswish.org.uk

A site that helps **bereaved** children and young people rebuild their lives after a family death. It offers support and guidance to families and anyone concerned about a **grieving** child.

REMEMBER
Here are some ways to help you say goodbye:

- Have a special place that you can visit. It could be a grave or a place that holds happy memories for you. You could even make this place somewhere in your garden.
- Hold a ceremony. Plan the way you'd like to say goodbye and pick music, poems or activities that will make it the occasion you want it to be.
- Do something in the person's honour. It could be raising money for charity, planting a tree, a plaque on a park bench or a piece in the paper.
- Write to them. Whether it's a short message, a long letter or a daily diary — write down what you'd like to share with them or tell them.
- Make a memory book and fill it with photos and family memories. Ask other family members to contribute.

SINGLE-PARENT FAMILIES

LIFE WITH ONE PARENT

Nearly one in four children live in lone-parent families. Over 90% of these live with their mother.

'I've never met my dad so I don't know any different.'

6 WAYS TO AN EASIER LIFE

HERE ARE SOME IDEAS FOR MAKING YOUR FAMILY LIFE RUN SMOOTHLY:

- If your parent is stressed out, do what you can to help.
- Know and accept the financial limitations, but think creatively about helping to overcome them.
- Look at your friends' families. Would you swap places? If not, why not?
- Don't dwell on the past. Think about the present or the future.
- Find friends in the same situation. You can support one another.
- Take on responsibility. The more you do the more capable you will become.

Lone parenting is now a very common thing. Mostly it occurs through divorce or bereavement, which means that one parent is left to raise the family on his or her own.

Whatever your family circumstances, life can often be more fun with one, particularly if the second carer was violent, aggressive, controlling or **manipulative**. But there can also be strains on a lone parent that don't exist to the same extent where parents share the load. A single parent can often feel pressured because they have to make all the decisions, especially if they don't have a strong support network around them.

'My mum, my sister and I are like three friends.'

Money could also be a worry. Without the financial contribution of another adult, it can leave a lone parent feeling **vulnerable** – if anything bad happens, how will they cope? But if the family income dramatically reduces through divorce or bereavement, this can be a real concern. You all need to adjust or change your lifestyle to match the reduced income and, as we all know, children aren't very understanding when they can't have the things they want! If you are solely dependant on one parent, you may worry that something bad might happen to them. When you've got two parents, you feel more secure because you have another loving parent to care for you.

But when you've only got one ... there is a lot of uncertainty. Finally, as the child of a lone parent, you may feel you have to grow up a bit faster than your friends who have a full complement of carers. It might be that your parent treats you more like another adult – confiding in you or asking advice. They may expect you to take more responsibility around the home, perhaps helping with younger **siblings** or doing household chores. The upside to all this is that you can be closer to a single parent – as close as friends.

YOU'RE NOT ALONE

Make a list of those people you could count on in difficult times:

1 YOUR OTHER PARENT?
If your other parent is around and you need help, they will no doubt be there for you.

2 SIBLINGS
Older brothers and sisters, whether they live with you or not, can be great to confide in and should give you lifelong support. Younger brothers and sisters can help around the house.

3 GRANDPARENTS OR AUNTS AND UNCLES
Often ready and willing to help out.

4 FAMILY FRIENDS/GODPARENTS
Close family friends are usually great in any crisis. They know you and your parent well and will be happy to help.

5 TEACHER/SCHOOL SUPPORT STAFF
With their extensive experience of helping children your age, they will give you solid advice and support. They know the right people to contact for anything from financial aid to home help.

6 YOUR FRIENDS
The very best people to keep you smiling. Along with their parents, they can also be of practical help.

7 NEIGHBOURS?
Because they live near, helping out shouldn't be an inconvenience. Any friendly neighbour would probably be happy to help.

JUST MUM AND I

Ben, 14, lives with his mum. He's never met his father. Usually it is fine, but his mum has fallen ill, which is hard on Ben.

There's just me and my mum, and most of the time I think we get on really well. She lets me do most of the stuff I want. We only argue if I want to do something when she's arranged for us to do something else.

> 'When she's ill, like now, it's really hard and I get worried that something's going to happen to her.'

I think there are probably less arguments because she doesn't have to discuss stuff with a third person. It's just up to her what I can or can't do. She doesn't have to say, 'Well, I don't mind but ask your father...' so I guess it's better that way, but then I've never known anything different. But when she's ill, like now, it's really hard and I get worried that something's going to happen to her. I'm having to do most of the chores. I do the shopping, the washing and cook our tea, so I don't see my friends much. I don't mind but what if Mum doesn't get better soon?

ASK THE EXPERTS...

Simon the social worker says...
It's often the case that single-parent families work together more effectively and share more than two-parent families. On the down side there isn't a spare parent handy in case something goes wrong. Talk to your mum about your worries and you may find she has already thought of these possibilities.

Anita the counsellor says...
It sounds like you and your mum have a really good, close relationship and I bet she appreciates your support. You can obviously see the benefits of only having one parent to negotiate with. Have you talked to Mum or anyone else who could reassure you about your worries over her health and your situation?

Mac the family liaison officer says...
It's great that you and your mum get on so well. It's perfectly understandable that you are concerned about her health and how it will impact on your freedom. Try voicing your concerns to your mum. She sounds like a pretty open person. If her illness is going to be ongoing, perhaps she could take on a part-time house-keeper to give you a hand?

MY DAD IS MY MUM

Alana, 15, lost her mum when she was young. Her dad copes just fine on his own.

I live with my dad because my mum died when we were little – I don't really remember her because I was only four.

I guess it's more unusual to be on your own with a dad rather than a mum, but it's all we know. Dad has a lot of support from both our grannies and so we've had a bit of female influence. There have been funny times, like when my sister started her period and both grans were away and she didn't want to tell Dad! Lou and I do more around the house than most of our friends. We have a routine over washing up and putting away, and we go with Dad to the supermarket every Friday evening – I don't think many of my friends go shopping with their mums anymore. I look at pictures of my mum – and Dad, Granny and Nan tell us things about her. They say I look more like her than Dad. Lou and I worry that Dad must be lonely – for years he didn't go out because he wanted to be there for us. I do appreciate what he's done for us, but sometimes I feel under pressure not to let him down and feel sad that when we leave home he'll be all on his own.

> 'I guess it's more unusual to be on your own with a dad rather than a mum.'

ASK THE EXPERTS...

Simon the social worker says...
Losing a parent leaves a gap that cries out to be filled. As a teenager you will have other commitments – such as friends, clubs, school-related activities and relationships – in addition to your family life. Juggling everything can become hard work. You may need to re-think how much you do for everyone. Talk to your dad about it. You never know, he might welcome a bit more time to himself!

Anita the counsellor says...
Your family sounds as though it has become very close since your mum died. Now that you and your sister are teenagers, it's only natural for you to be developing some independence. This could apply to your dad, too. Maybe it's time to use that closeness to open some discussion with him about all your plans for the future.

Mac the family liaison officer says...
It's lovely that you care so much about your dad's happiness. He is lucky to have daughters who are so helpful. I'm sure he's well aware that as teenagers, you and your sister will want to go out more and that your needs will be changing. You might be surprised – as you need your dad less, you might find him pursuing his own interests and making new friends.

WE'VE NEVER GOT ANY MONEY

Michael, 13, lives with his mum. She works hard and would like to buy Michael more, but there's never enough money.

I don't remember my dad being around – he lives in London now and I hardly ever see him. It's okay being on my own with mum. The only problem is we never seem to have any money!

If my dad had stuck around there probably would have been more money for everything. My mum works hard and she'd like to give me more stuff, but she just doesn't earn that much. Sometimes she's wiped out because she's got to do everything on her own, but she says having a bloke around would only make life more difficult! She's had some boyfriends but she could never tolerate them for long. I don't think my life is that different from my mates who've got two parents. Some of them don't have any money either, or their dad drinks it all. One mate's dad spends it all on the horses – so I think I'm better off without that.

> 'If my dad had stuck around there probably would have been more money for everything.'

ASK THE EXPERTS...

Simon the social worker says...
The closeness and sharing that comes from having one parent can make up for having less money. Think about what sort of parent you would want to be. Would it be most important to you to be able to give children lots of money and gifts? Or is it more important to spend time with them and be involved in their lives? Now what sort of children would you want to help you make that happen?!

Anita the counsellor says...
Your mum is obviously caring and independent and has brought you up to be the same. You sound mature in recognizing that not all kids from two-parent families have a lot of money spent on them either! At least your mum would like to be able to give you more and works hard for what you do have.

Mac the family liaison officer says...
It can be frustrating when you never seem to have any money. However, as you've recognized, things could be worse. Have you thought about getting a part-time job yourself, such as a newspaper or lawn-mowing round? You say your Mum is often wiped out — maybe you could do a bit to help her around the house?

THE OUTCOMES

After reading our experts' advice, Ben, Alana and Michael wrote back to let us know how things turned out...

GET CONNECTED

FOLLOW THIS WEB LINK TO FIND OUT MORE:

www.teengrowth.com

A health website that offers information and advice on puberty, family, friends, drugs, sex and emotions.

CASE STUDY 1

Find support

Mum got worse but my aunt and Mum's friends came to help out so it wasn't all suddenly down to me. I had to do a lot of the chores and the shopping, but my aunt sorted out all the bills. Thank goodness! Mum was worried about the heating and phone getting cut off. She's on the mend now and she might be able to go back to work in a couple of weeks. It really scared me though – like, REALLY scared me.

CASE STUDY 2

Don't take it all on

I didn't think that Dad might actually want a bit more time to himself. I've been so busy worrying that he'll be lonely, rather than thinking whether he likes to be alone. Dad told me that he's quite happy with things as they are. He knows Lou and I are growing up and he said he's proud that we are such loving and responsible daughters! He said we've all got our own lives to lead. If he wanted to meet someone he probably could but he's not keen on getting back into the dating scene – not yet anyway.

CASE STUDY 3

Appreciate what you have

I guess the bottom line is that I respect my mum, so I don't feel resentful about not having much. She does her best to pay for things. I wouldn't swap with my friends. Mum trusts me and gives me freedom, even if she can't give me other stuff. I just can't wait until I'm old enough to work and earn my own money.

REMEMBER

- It can be more fun with one – you may have a very close bond with your parent.
- If you're worried about having no back-up, make a list of the people around who you can rely on.
- If your parent is stressed and moody, do what you can to help out.
- Appreciate what you do have.

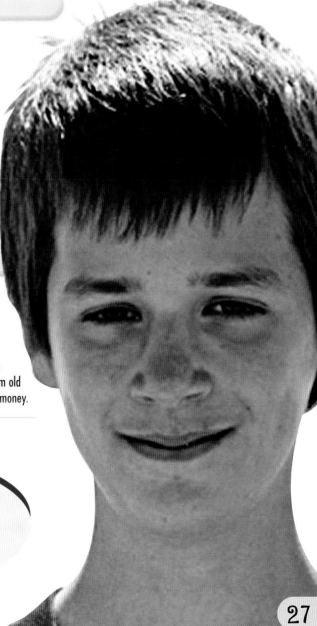

DATING PARENTS: THE GOOD vs. THE BAD

THE GOOD

- Your parent is happier
- Your parent is more relaxed
- Your parent has more support
- You like your parent's boyfriend/girlfriend
- You do different, interesting things together
- No more guilt about leaving your parent alone

THE BAD

- Your parent is more emotional
- Your parent spends less time with you
- Not liking your parent's boyfriend/girlfriend
- Having to do things you don't want to do
- Feeling uncomfortable in your own home
- Being told what to do by a stranger

If the bad outweighs the good – then it might help to talk to someone outside of the family. A friend or an adult you trust might be able to reassure you. If the problem runs deeper, then you can always contact one of the organizations on p. 47.

PARENTAL DATING
WHEN PARENTS PLAY THE DATING GAME

It is human nature for all of us to want to be loved and share our lives with someone – and that includes single parents.

If your parent is single or your parents are separated or divorced, you might have to face another experience that friends of two-parent families miss out on – that of your parents dating. It might be something you're brought up with and so it doesn't seem odd, but it can feel odd or make you angry.

Let's face it, nothing makes us cringe more than seeing grown-ups in love. But, it's also fair to remember that most adults want to have a significant other to share their life with. You may even find that you're feeling jealous or sidelined.

'I wish they weren't all soppy in front of me.'

This is natural. You've had Mum or Dad all to yourself and suddenly they are spending time and giving attention to someone else, probably a complete stranger to you. And you may be forced to get to know this stranger. The key to successfully surviving the parental dating game is – as usual – communication. If you're feeling neglected, tell your parent that they need to find time to spend with you, too. If you are feeling annoyed with their behaviour, talk about boundaries. If you can't handle your mum snogging on the couch with her new boyfriend while you're trying to watch *EastEnders*, tell her! Don't do it in front of the boyfriend as this will lead to embarrassment all round. Leave it for when you have Mum on her own and then discuss it with her. But if you are worried that your dad might love his girlfriend more than you, let him know how you feel.

Your parent probably feels they deserve to have a life outside of the family, just as you do with friends and school. If you understand this and treat them with consideration, they may return the courtesy and involve you in any big decisions they might be trying to make.

'When he's around, Mum's a lot less stressed with us.'

10 UNOFFICIAL RULES FOR DATING PARENTS

Your parents are great at laying down rules for you or offering you advice about anything and everything. Here are some of the rules you could suggest to them:

1 Under no circumstances should you snog in front of me.

2 Act your age. Leave the teenage behaviour to me.

3 Be yourself. You're great as you are so don't try to change to suit your new love interest.

4 Don't borrow my clothes.

5 Don't neglect me in favour of your new boyfriend/girlfriend. I still need you and want to spend time with you.

6 Don't take dating too seriously. Have fun! You deserve it.

7 Only bring home someone you would really like to meet me.

8 Don't discuss anything intimate. I don't want to know.

9 If it's getting serious, I want to know.

10 Please listen to my point of view. It's affecting my life, too.

29

I GAVE HIM HELL

Katy, 16, remembers when her mum first started seeing Brian. She couldn't and wouldn't accept him.

'I thought, "Who the hell does he think he is?" He's not my dad.'

When my mum started seeing Brian, my sister and I made his life hell! Our dad had died two years before and I felt we didn't need anyone else.

My sister got over Brian's arrival quicker because she was at Art College during the week. I was the one left at home with the pair of them. When Brian moved in I thought, 'Who the hell does he think he is? He's not my dad!' In a weird way I was blaming him for the fact that Dad wasn't around. Brian would come into the house and my sister and I wouldn't even say hello until Mum forced us. I spent the first year hiding in my room. I ate upstairs in front of the TV with my dinner on my lap while they ate at the table downstairs. Mum gave up trying to make me. Mum used to get annoyed with me but she didn't understand how angry I felt. And I kind of hated her too. I felt like she'd betrayed me – we only needed each other, we didn't need HIM around.

ASK THE EXPERTS...

Simon the social worker says...
It's great when families pull together to support each other through bad times. But when time has passed, you can lose a bit of that closeness as people get on with their lives again. It hurts if you're the last one left not quite ready to move on. So, try letting the others know if you need them to stick around a bit longer. Think of things you'd enjoy doing together that would give you that closeness and support again.

Anita the counsellor says...
It must have been very hard for you coming to terms with losing your dad and having someone new enter such a close family unit. Brian must care a lot about your mum and be very committed to her, because it sounds like he's been extremely patient and understanding with you and your sister. It could be helpful to tell your mum about your feelings and express your anger in a different way.

Mac the family liaison officer says...
Losing your dad would have been devastating for your mum, too. But, you want your mum to be happy, don't you? Brian might be a really nice guy – but you won't know unless you try getting to know him a little bit. Neither he, nor anyone else for that matter, could ever replace your dad. Try not to think of him as some kind of father figure and just a friend who makes your mum happy.

WE WANTED TO BE BRIDESMAIDS

Stella, 14, became really fond of her mum's boyfriend. She thought they would get married.

My mum and dad split when I was really little, so I don't really remember Dad.

Mum had a few boyfriends when we were growing up, but didn't really involve us in any of that too much. I guess as we got older she found it a bit harder to keep her relationships from us, so when she met Del, she didn't want to hide it. I remember when he first came round, Mum was being all silly and girly and Nadia and I thought, 'What's with her?' I didn't know what to think of Del then. But the more he came round, the more we liked him – he was funny and easy to talk to, and he organized really nice things for us to do. Nadia and I hoped Mum and Del would get married – we liked him that much! We were really surprised and upset when Mum said they were splitting up. Nadia actually cried! When I asked why, Mum said, 'Sometimes there isn't really a reason.' Great answer, Mum!

> 'I didn't know what to think of Del then. He seemed okay, but not amazing.'

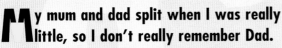

ASK THE EXPERTS...

Simon the social worker says...
It's hard enough to predict how your own love life is going to turn out let alone someone else's. And it's not just your parent who takes an emotional risk when they start a new relationship. It's natural to find yourself getting used to and liking your parent's new partner. So if you catch yourself imagining how things might turn out, maybe it's time to talk to your mum and get a reality check!

Anita the counsellor says...
Your mum was protective of you when you were little but that gets harder to do as life goes on. She may be able to explain things better to you when she's less upset herself and understanding more may make things less painful. Are you able to keep in touch with Del yourself since you had such a good relationship with him?

Mac the family liaison officer says...
It's a shame that things didn't work out for your mum and Del – but better they end their relationship now than stay together for the wrong reasons. Think of this as your first lesson in learning how to let go of someone. The fact is, Del wasn't the right one for your mum. Chances are she'll find someone else really nice in time.

CASE STUDY 3

SHE GETS ON MY NERVES

Wes, 12, lives with his dad and is used to him having girlfriends. Most of the time it's not a problem, but dad's new girlfriend is becoming a pain.

> 'You can tell she "disapproves" of some of the things I do or say. She gives me a look that makes me want to tell her where to get off.'

My dad's had a few girlfriends and most of them have been all right. But now he's seeing this woman that really gets on my nerves.

It seems like she comes over every day or is giving my dad a hard time if he can't see her. She even complained when dad had to go to a parents' evening. It wasn't as if he was out enjoying himself.

You can tell she 'disapproves' of some of the things I do or say. She gives me a look that makes me want to tell her where to get off, but my dad would be furious with me if I ever did that. And she's always telling my dad what to do, too. She says things like 'Why do you keep that there?' when it's always been there and it's not been a problem for dad and I for the last three years! She just wants to rule dad's life.

ASK THE EXPERTS...

Simon the social worker says...
Having someone new come into your home can be unsettling at the best of times. When they come in bursting with fresh ideas and different views, **it can be very frustrating.** The reality is though that everyone has their own ideas and views about family life. And anyone who goes on to join your family will make their own mark. At least with strong individuals, you know where you stand from the start!

Anita the counsellor says...
It's good to hear that you've been accepting of your dad's relationships in the past. It sounds like this time, it's **just a bit of a personailty clash.** As you've accepted his relationships in the past he will probably be **sympathetic** to your feelings, if you explain that you have a problem with this woman's behaviour and that it's upsetting you.

Mac the family liaison officer says...
It's to your credit that you have been biting your tongue around your dad's **girlfriend rather than saying things you know will upset her.** Chances are, your dad's girlfriend is probably feeling insecure and is finding it just as hard to work out how to be with you. Try chatting with her on her own and see if she relaxes with you a bit more.

THE OUTCOMES

After reading our experts' advice, Katy, Stella and Wes wrote back to let us know how things turned out...

C A S E   S T U D Y   1

Think of others

Now I'm about to go off to college and I'm quite glad Mum's got someone. It's taken me a while to get used to it but Brian has never tried to replace my dad and he's never tried to tell me what to do. But the truth is, my mum needed more than just us kids, she needed a partner too. I think it might have been easier if Mum had asked if I minded, or had even said,

'I know you mind but I need this...' That never happened – it didn't matter that it was my house too, and that it had been my dad's house. But I suppose now I've had a bit more time to get over Dad. I still miss him and wish he was around to talk to, but at least I've still got Mum (and Brian!) when some people haven't even got anybody. I guess I should be grateful for that.

C A S E   S T U D Y   2

Don't expect too much

Nadia and I tried to keep in touch with Del but it was all a bit too weird so we sort of stopped making the effort. I think Mum was quite relieved. If I see Del in town, I say hello, and maybe even have a chat and a coffee, but I guess even that'll fizzle out over time. I do

miss him a bit and I miss Mum being all happy and everything. I think the next boyfriend she has will get a hard time because we'll compare him to Del. Not only that, but we won't want to get so close to anyone again, because it's upsetting when they're gone.

GET CONNECTED

FOLLOW THESE WEB LINKS TO FIND OUT MORE:

www.bbc.co.uk/teens

This BBC website is an excellent teen site covering everything from entertainment to life issues. Check out the 'Real Life' in the 'Girls' section and 'Life' in the 'Lads' section of the website.

www.kidzworld.com

An American magazine-style website with games, news, entertainment and gossip. There's plenty of advice and you can write in with your own problems.

REMEMBER
- This isn't about you. It's about your mum or dad wanting the love of another adult. Their love for you won't change.
- Try to think of your parent's feelings – you want them to be happy, don't you?
- If something doesn't feel right or if you are unhappy, talk to them about it.
- If it's hard talking to them, talk to someone else.

C A S E   S T U D Y   3

Talking helps

I found it hard to start a conversation with Dad about it but one day he asked me what was up. He'd asked so I told him. I said she was really getting on my nerves. He said, 'She's getting on my nerves too!' So then he dumped her, which was fine by me!

STEPFAMILIES

STRANGERS OR A BRAND NEW FAMILY?

Of the one in four children whose parents get divorced, half of them will see their parents remarry or find a new partner to form a stepfamily.

Many people have families extended through the new relationship or remarriage of one or both parents. Being attached to another family because of your parent's love life can be difficult to deal with. They are strangers who suddenly become part of your family life and you are forced to get to know them. Remember, being a stepparent is tricky too – at first they might be twitchy and uncomfortable around you or overly keen for you to like them. It's the same with stepsisters and stepbrothers; you never know how your relationship is going to grow.

You may find that you've got a new best mate in the making or you could feel like you've just acquired a prize geek for a family member. Equally when a new baby comes along and you've suddenly got a half-brother or half-sister, it can feel exciting and special, but you may also feel that you don't want to share your parent with anymore people. You could have the problem of your step**siblings** being treated differently to you.

I HATE THEM, WHAT CAN I DO?

As a child you are dependent on your parents but may have no influence on some decisions they make. If you are deeply unhappy, talk to them and tell them. If you don't feel able to do that, or if you have done so and nothing changes, try talking to someone else. There is a lot of help out there for you – just look at p. 47 for all the people you can contact.

'I didn't want them to come and live with us.'

If you feel they get away with murder while you are given a hard time about every little thing you do, then it's easy to **resent** both the other kids and your stepparent. All relationships take effort and time. Everyone is trying to find the right balance, so you need to make it clear what roles you're happy for your stepparent to play in the parenting of you. It's important to keep talking to your real parent. If you make an effort to get along with everyone, you may find that you have a newly formed, different-shaped, happy family.

'I hate having to explain my family to people.'

5 THINGS TO THINK ABOUT IF IT'S HAPPENING TO YOU

Settling in to a new family situation is hard for every child. Here's some things to keep in mind...

1 YOU'VE GOT A LOT TO DEAL WITH
Because nothing is as it used to be, you will have a lot on your mind. Try not to let your school work or your friendships suffer. Dwell on your family issues outside of school so you can stay focused in school. Talk to your teachers and friends so they know what's on your mind.

2 KEEP TALKING TO YOUR PARENT
If you have problems with your stepfamily, talk to your parent about it. Choose your moment carefully, when you are having one-on-one time and don't criticise or blame the others. Work out a solution together.

3 DON'T MAKE IT MORE DIFFICULT
*It's easy to be grumpy, unco-operative or moody, and it's understandable at first. But refusing to join in will just cause **conflict**.*

4 ACCEPT THE SITUATION
You may not have wanted it, you may not have even been consulted, but if your parent has made the decision to be with someone, you need to accept it.

5 ALL RELATIONSHIPS TAKE EFFORT
If you put in the effort, you'll get to know your stepparent or stepfamily more quickly and they will get to know you. Hopefully at least you'll find you CAN live with them.

I FEEL LIKE A SLAVE

Ed, 14, is having problems with his stepdad but he doesn't want to say anything.

My stepdad just treats me like a slave. He's always saying, 'Ed can you get that?' even when it's something right next to him. I just look annoyed and do it usually. I don't think he notices how annoyed it makes me.

Sometimes I say 'no' but he just laughs. He's always sending me to the shops for stuff and the other day he made me order an Indian meal for everyone and then he said I'd got it

'I wanted to shout at him but it wouldn't have got me anywhere. He would have laughed at me.'

wrong and had to do it again. I wanted to shout at him, 'Why didn't you just do it yourself in the first place?' but it wouldn't have got me anywhere. He would have laughed at me and then everyone else would have laughed too. I already felt an idiot so I didn't say anything.

ASK THE EXPERTS...

Simon the social worker says...
Getting a new stepparent can be an exciting time loaded with expectation. But when someone regularly treats you in a nasty way, then you have a problem. And it isn't down to you to sort the person out. Get into the habit of standing up for yourself (without being rude), say 'no' when you are uncomfortable with the situation — try walking away and doing something you like instead.

Anita the counsellor says...
Maybe your stepdad is lazy and insensitive or maybe he's trying to include you and thinks you're used to this level of responsibility. If it's hard to talk to him about how you're feeling, try bringing it up with your mum and seeing if this helps. If not, talk to another adult about the situation and seek guidance on how to be assertive about your right to be respected.

Mac the family liaison officer says...
It certainly sounds like your new stepdad is quite tough on you. It's up to you to show him that you don't want to be pushed around. Practice with your friends how you could have handled the situation with the Indian takeaways. Try some other scenarios. Then, next time it happens, you should be able to stand up for yourself (without being disrespectful) and emerge from the experience with dignity.

I DON'T FEEL LIKE HIS SON ANYMORE

Tom, 12, can't bear his dad's new wife and her kids. He feels like a nuisance when he goes there.

I hate my stepfamily. My dad only lives up the road, but I don't want to go there as I don't want to see the rest of them!

My dad's wife, Vanessa, is such a cow and her kids are just total spoilt brats. There are two of them – Rory and Maddy. Their dad died when they were little and I think Vanessa's been trying to make up for it ever since. And it makes

> 'I just feel like I've turned up and spoiled everything.'

me sick the way my dad just jumps at whatever she says and buys them anything they want. One of my friends said I was jealous, but I don't think it's that. If they were nicer people, I might not mind. Vanessa's a clean freak. All I hear is, 'Have you washed your hands?... We don't have food in the bedrooms... We don't put our feet on the furniture.' Okay, I get the picture. I feel like an unwelcome guest, not like a son. They're all together – this nice, polite family – and I feel like I've turned up and spoiled everything.

ASK THE EXPERTS...

Simon the social worker says... Having two families can mean you have to deal with two different sets of household rules and parenting styles. That doesn't mean you should give up on your dad's new family completely though. Perhaps it signals a need for you to do some adapting when you're in their house. At the same time, to some degree, they need to learn to take you as you are. Try explaining your feelings to your dad.

Anita the counsellor says... It sounds like you've got a lot of strong feelings which are stopping you making the most of your stepfamily. Can you talk to Dad when you're alone? It can be hard to adjust to the different standards between the two homes. You still have two parents who love you and your dad shows you this by inviting you to his new home and with the little gifts and money at special times.

Mac the family liaison officer says... It might be worth giving some thought to what your dad sees in Vanessa. And try getting to know your step siblings a bit better. There might be more to them than meets the eye. Also, try talking to your dad about how left out you feel when you go round there. If you are reasonable and mature in the way you discuss the situation, you should get an understanding response from him.

WE'VE GOT TWO HOMES

Jessie and Sara (14 and 15) have adjusted to life with two homes.

Mum's boyfriend, Alex, is really, really moody, but then he always has been.

As for our (sort of) stepmum, Narinder, we more or less met her when she was moving in with us and so we had to accept her. We couldn't have told my dad we didn't like her. But actually we do like her. Jessie was really quiet at first and it was a bit of a battle of wills, but now, Narinder's just like another mum – we even give her presents for Mother's Day.

It's cool having two homes – except we don't know where our stuff is half the time! We do it on a day-by-day basis, which is what we wanted. We felt it was better than having a week with one and week with the other or only seeing Dad at weekends. This way we get to see them both equally. One drops us off in the morning and the other picks us up in the evening. It only gets tricky when we have arguments. Birthdays are difficult and we don't know what to do about Christmas. Both our parents want us to be with them and we want to see both of them, too.

> 'We couldn't have told my Dad we didn't like her. But actually we do.'

ASK THE EXPERTS...

Simon the social worker says... Some families move with the changes and take in new people really easily. Everybody gets on with life and gets by with each other. Arguments still happen though when we express ourselves and if you're always on the move you need to be creative about sorting them out. Phoning, texting and email can keep communication going when you're apart.

Anita the counsellor says... You two are lucky that your parents and their partners have been willing to be flexible about arrangements. It is good to hear that you appreciate Narinder and that she's made the effort although it may have been a bit difficult to begin with. It is a compliment to you all that everyone would like to have each other's company at Christmas and in this spirit it's likely that you'll work something out between you.

Mac the family liaison officer says... It sounds like you and your sister have come a long way in adjusting to your new family situation. If you have a problem with your mum's boyfriend's attitude, you should try talking to your mum about it. She might be able to have a quiet word with him on their own so it's not awkward for anyone. It sounds as though you've got a living arrangement that suits everyone which is great.

THE OUTCOMES

After reading our experts' advice, Ed, Tom and Sara let us know how things turned out...

GET CONNECTED

FOLLOW THESE WEB LINKS TO FIND OUT MORE:

www.parentlineplus.org.uk

The children and young people's section of this site tells you what to expect when your parents divorce.

www.stepfamilies.co.uk

Mostly a support site for adults, but there is Kidstep for kids to ask questions and a forum to leave messages or start discussions with others.

C A S E   S T U D Y   1

Discuss your problems

It was really weird because I decided to tell my mum that my stepdad was really bugging me. Her reaction wasn't what I expected. I expected her to feel sorry for me. She said I'd sit on my backside all day if I wasn't asked to help and that I shouldn't resent it. She said I wouldn't be so annoyed if it wasn't my stepdad asking. I guess that bit is true. If Mum was the one asking, I wouldn't have even thought about it. But she obviously told him what I'd said because he had a chat with me about and actually said sorry!

REMEMBER
- The more effort you make, the more quickly you will get to know your stepfamily.
- You don't have to love them, you just have to live with them.
- It's an unsettling time for everyone, not just you. It should get easier.
- Accept that your life has changed and try to be positive – things may just turn out fine!

C A S E   S T U D Y   2

It's your life

It's not so bad now, because I'm a bit older and I've got a choice. Up until I was about 11, my mum and dad tried to make me go over there to stay, but now I just say if I don't want to go. I see Dad on his own at football. He does get upset with me that I don't go round more, but I just can't get on with them and I don't need to be made to feel uncomfortable. Vanessa doesn't make an effort, so why should I? I think she's pleased I don't go round there much.

C A S E   S T U D Y   3

Find solutions

We didn't have anything to worry about really. It all worked out fine. We spent Christmas Eve at Dad's, and opened our presents there. Then we met Mum and Alex in the pub for a drink and then went home with Mum. We realize we are lucky: our parents have made a real effort to stay friends – we've never witnessed any kind of battles. We don't feel scarred by their break up at all.

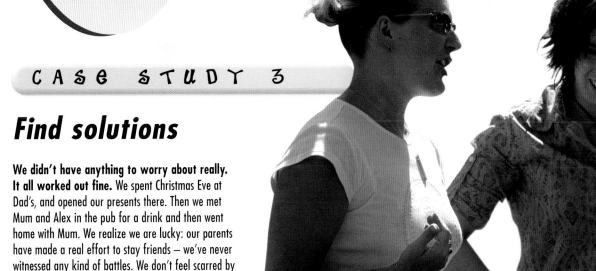

VIOLENT FAMILIES

WHEN VIOLENCE IS IN YOUR HOME

'I want it to stop but I can't talk to anyone or my family might split up.'

Abuse can come in different forms – physical, sexual or emotional. There are over half a million reported incidents a year in the UK.

STAY SAFE

- Don't get caught up in a fight.
- Find a safe place and stay there.
- Talk to your non-violent parent to try to get them to seek help.
- Talk to someone you trust, such as a teacher, family friend or family liaison officer at your school.
- Call the police.
- Call a children's helpline.
- Find help for you and your family. Here's where to start (there are more organizations listed on p. 43).

(Calls are free and will not show up on your bill.)

FOR YOU
Childline 0800 1111
NSPCC 0808 800 5000

FOR YOUR PARENT
Women's Aid
England 01279 83 66 11
N Ireland 028 90 331818
Scotland 0131 475 2372
Wales 029 20390874

FOR VIOLENT MEN
Everyman Project
020 7737 6747
(for counselling and advice)

Your home should be the safest place of all and however complicated your family circumstances, it's the role of your parents to make you feel protected and loved. But for some children, home can be a place where you experience violence and abuse.

If you are living with domestic violence, it can be extremely distressing. If your father hits your mother, you may feel sad and confused – how should you feel towards him? You may love him and fear him at the same time. And if he's violent towards your mother, he might also be violent towards you. It may be that you're living with verbal abuse, or even sexual abuse. You may feel shame and not want anyone to know what goes on at home. You may feel anger at the abuser and the one being abused – why can't she stand up to him or do something about it? Whatever the circumstances, there is no excuse for domestic violence. You may feel it is up to you to protect your parent or that you can do something to stop the violence.

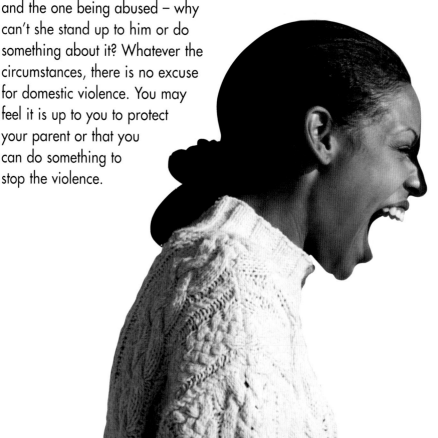

40

> 'I tell my mum to leave but she says I don't understand.'

If you do try to protect them, you risk being injured or verbally abused yourself. You are powerless to stop a violent person from being violent, but you can get help. Try talking to your non-violent parent first. They may even believe that you don't know it is happening – if they row downstairs while you're supposed to be asleep. But sometimes there can be a pretence on the part of your parents or other family members that it is not happening. This can be incredibly difficult for you as your confused, angry, anxious feeling can never go away. Domestic violence is often a secret, untalked-about problem that can have a lasting and devastating effect on the children involved. Your school work could suffer. You may feel stressed, fearful or depressed. You may even feel violent towards others. So if you are suffering from a disturbing family 'secret', there are places to get help. Pick up the phone and talk to someone.

WHY DOESN'T SHE LEAVE HIM?

There are any number of reasons why a woman stays with a violent man. Here are some possibilities:

- *She's too scared to leave.*
- *She can't think of anywhere to go.*
- *She has no money.*
- *She's worried about losing her home.*
- *She doesn't want to put her children through such upheaval.*
- *She's so ground down by the abuse that she doesn't have the energy.*
- *The abuser is **manipulative** and convinces her to stay.*

BREAK THE CYCLE

In the US, 79% of violent children have witnessed violence between their parents. And 75% of all abusive men watched their fathers beating their mothers. Witnessing violence is traumatic but continuing that cycle is tragic. If you have strong feelings of anger, you need to get some help. Don't be a victim of violence anymore. Break the cycle by going to your GP who can refer you to the right professional to talk to.

DRINK MADE HIM VIOLENT

Tara, 13, was living with her mum's violent boyfriend, until they escaped to a refuge.

> 'We felt really guilty because we wanted to help Mum.'

Mum has been single since I was about five and my little brother, Bradley, was three. When she met Terry, he was really nice. After about three months he moved in with us and then almost overnight it changed. If he'd been out drinking, he started hitting Mum.

Bradley and I were always in bed when it happened, but we could hear it and we were really scared. We'd both be crying and would get into bed together. We felt guilty because we wanted to help Mum, but we were scared in case he turned on us. Afterwards he'd be nice again and bring us all presents. Even when everything was okay we were nervous it might happen again. One night, we heard the usual arguing and then a big crash. We were so scared for Mum, but suddenly she was shouting up the stairs, telling us we were leaving. Terry tried to block our way but Mum pushed past him. We ran into the street and kept running until we were sure he wasn't coming after us. Then Mum called the police. They found us a refuge for the night and said they would find us a safe house to live in. I'm scared I'll never see our home or friends again.

ASK THE EXPERTS...

Simon the social worker says...
A violent family member can be a terrifying thing to live with. You may feel you never know when he's going to blow his top and lash out. Excess alcohol consumption can often be a trigger for this kind of behaviour in some people. Whatever the reason, violence should never be tolerated. Your mum has been very brave to take you and your brother away from Terry. Things will get better from here.

Anita the counsellor says...
I'm not surprised how frightened you and Bradley were and there's no need for you to feel guilty – you couldn't have protected your mum. She has done the right thing in getting you away from that situation, which must have taken courage. If you are troubled by these events in the future it could be a good idea to find someone to talk to about your feelings.

Mac the family liaison officer says...
This has been a tough situation for you, Bradley and your Mum to get through – but you've done it! Remember, there was nothing you and Bradley could have done to help your mum. The important thing now is to look ahead and feel positive about the future. The material things you've left behind don't matter. Much more important is that the three of you are okay and no longer have to endure the violence.

THE OUTCOME

Tara told us how things turned out...

CASE STUDY 1

Be free of fear

I didn't know what a safe house would be like. I thought it would be like a hospital ward or something, and we'd have to sleep with lots of other people. But when we got there it was okay. We had a little room and shared a kitchen. After a few days I actually quite liked being there with other kids my age. It was easy to make friends quite quickly.

We stayed in the safe house for two months until we got re-housed and I'm pretty sure Terry's out of our lives forever. I think Mum will be really scared of having another relationship, but I think I've learned something from it, I actually feel stronger and I don't think I'd ever let anyone push me around like that.

GET CONNECTED

FOLLOW THESE WEB LINKS TO FIND OUT MORE:

www.bbc.co.uk/health/hh

This section of the BBC website is called Hitting Home and covers every aspect of domestic violence.

www.womensroom.org

This site is for mothers and their children suffering from domestic violence. There are specific pages for kids and teens.

www.childline.org.uk

The website of the national children's helpline.

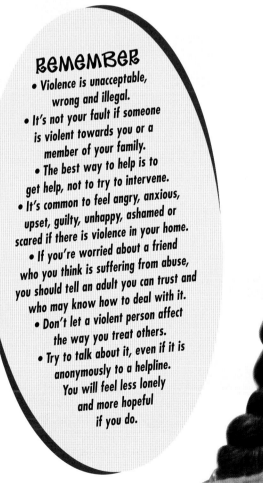

REMEMBER
- Violence is unacceptable, wrong and illegal.
- It's not your fault if someone is violent towards you or a member of your family.
- The best way to help is to get help, not to try to intervene.
- It's common to feel angry, anxious, upset, guilty, unhappy, ashamed or scared if there is violence in your home.
- If you're worried about a friend who you think is suffering from abuse, you should tell an adult you can trust and who may know how to deal with it.
- Don't let a violent person affect the way you treat others.
- Try to talk about it, even if it is anonymously to a helpline. You will feel less lonely and more hopeful if you do.

TROUBLESOME TEEN OR GOLDEN CHILD?

See where you fit in to your fabulously functional or dysfunctional family by following this flow chart...

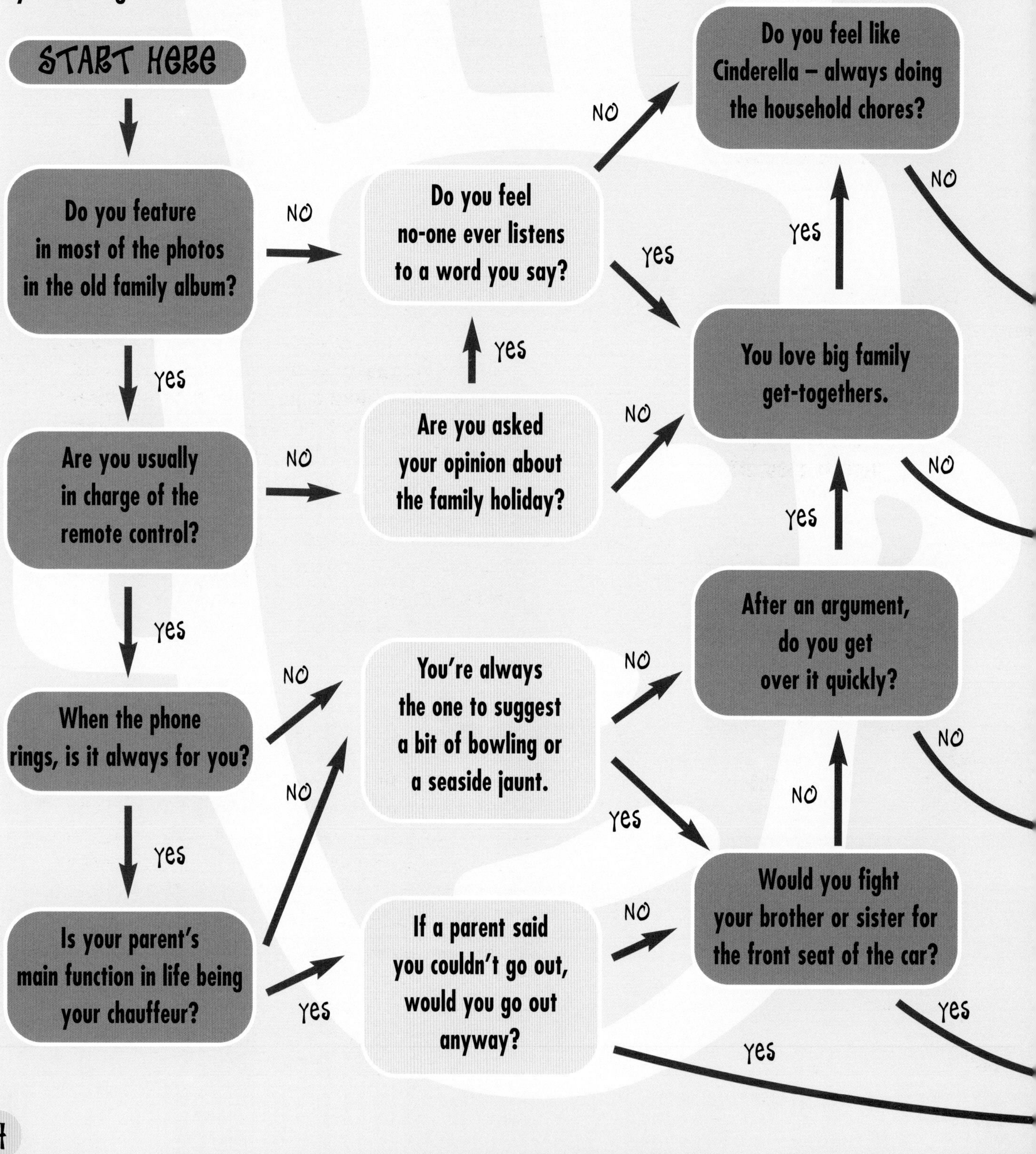

START HERE

Do you feature in most of the photos in the old family album?

NO →

Do you feel no-one ever listens to a word you say?

NO →

Do you feel like Cinderella – always doing the household chores?

YES

Are you usually in charge of the remote control?

NO →

Are you asked your opinion about the family holiday?

YES ↑

YES

You love big family get-togethers.

YES

When the phone rings, is it always for you?

NO →

You're always the one to suggest a bit of bowling or a seaside jaunt.

NO →

After an argument, do you get over it quickly?

NO

NO

YES

Is your parent's main function in life being your chauffeur?

YES →

If a parent said you couldn't go out, would you go out anyway?

NO →

Would you fight your brother or sister for the front seat of the car?

YES

YES

NO

YES

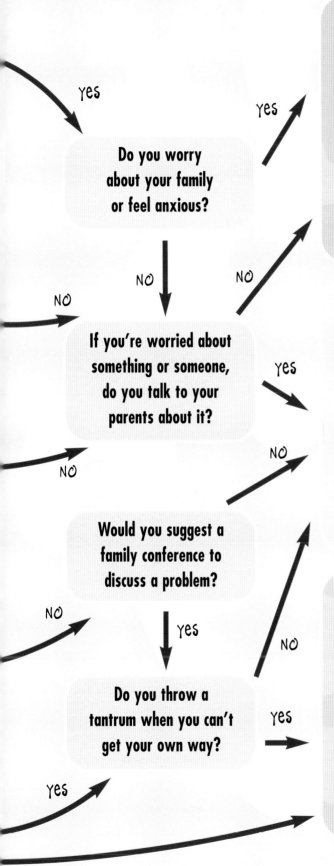

yes

Do you worry about your family or feel anxious?

yes

NO

NO

NO

If you're worried about something or someone, do you talk to your parents about it?

yes

NO

NO

Would you suggest a family conference to discuss a problem?

NO

yes

NO

Do you throw a tantrum when you can't get your own way?

yes

yes

THE TROUBLED TEEN

It's okay to have a sensitive side and to be a bit introverted. But don't be sidelined by other members of your family who shout louder or seem to have needs greater than your own. You have opinions worth listening to and you have worries worth talking about, so let your parents know that you'd like to have your say. Your happiness is just as important as everyone else's, so do yourself a favour and speak up.

THE CHERISHED CHILD

Well, aren't you a good one to have around? You're happy in your skin, confident and relaxed. You have a point of view but don't feel the need to hammer it home at every opportunity. You like equality and strive for fairness within your family. You're a good communicator and have no problem talking about your troubles with others. You try to make like easy for your parents and generally enjoy family life. All in all life around you is a breeze!

BOSSY BOOTS

So, you think the universe revolves around you, do you? Or is it just that your family should? In your quest to have your needs met you seem to forget that other people might have things they like to do, too. If you expect your parents to accommodate your busy social life, or your siblings to fit in with your demands, then maybe it's time you took others into account. Remember, often it's nicer to give than to receive. Try it – it might feel good!

BALLISTIC *a common expression used when someone erupts or explodes in anger. The word relates to ballistic missile – a missile that is fired into the air at such a force as to maintain a given speed and keep on a chosen path.*

BEREAVED OR BEREAVEMENT *to have lost someone you love through death*

COMPROMISE *to settle a dispute by both giving a bit to the other. Meeting half way.*

CONFLICT *be at odds with something. To clash, argue or fight.*

EMPOWERED *to feel you have control and authority to make decisions*

EXPECTATIONS *something hoped for or looked forward to. Parents' expectations for their children are usually what they hope their children will achieve.*

FOSTERED *to be looked after temporarily by people other than your natural or adoptive parents*

GRIEF OR GRIEVING *the deeply sad and distressed feeling that many people have after the death of someone they love. Grief is an intense and long-lasting feeling.*

IRRATIONAL *not logical or rational, defies reason, cannot easily be explained*

MANIPULATIVE *to be clever, skillful or devious in getting others to do what you want them to do. To influence someone in an indirect or underhand way.*

MORTALITY *the awareness of being mortal, knowing you are going to die, that your life is going to end at sometime in the future*

NUCLEAR FAMILY *traditional social unit of parents and their children living together as a family*

PHILOSOPHICAL *dealing with problems with a calm, level-headed outlook*

RESENT OR RESENTFUL *to feel bitter and upset about something or someone. A deep feeling that something is unjust or someone is being unfair.*

SENSITIVE *to have regard for the feelings of others. To be thoughtful towards other people. To be easily offended or upset.*

SIBLINGS *brothers and sisters. Children of the same parents.*

SUCCESSION *a chain, one thing following another which follows another, with no foreseen end*

SYMPATHETIC OR SYMPATHY *show understanding towards another*

VULNERABLE *to be capable of being hurt or wounded. To feel open and exposed to harm, temptation, or the influence of others.*

THE GET REAL ADVICE DIRECTORY

If you've got a problem and you'd like to talk to a trained professional or counsellor, here are some useful numbers. Don't suffer in silence. These helplines are there to help you and you don't have to give your name.

HELPLINES

ANTI-BULLYING CAMPAIGN 020 738 1446
Advice on anything to do with bullying.

CHILDLINE 0800 1111
www.childline.org.uk
For help with any worries or problems.

KIDSCAPE 08451 205204
www.kidscape.org.uk
For help with bullying or abuse.

NSPCC 0808 8005000
www.worriedneed2talk.org.uk
A free counselling and advice line.

THE LINE 0800 2797454
Free counselling for teenagers.

THE SAMARITANS 08457 909090
www.samaritans.org
For help with any worries or problems.

YOUTH 2 YOUTH 0208 8963675
Emotional advice from young people.

OTHER ORGANIZATIONS

AUSTRALIAN DRUG FOUNDATION
www.adf.org.au
The Australian Drug Foundation has a wide range of information on all aspects of drugs, their effects and their legal position in Australia.

CRUSE BEREAVEMENT
www.rd4u.org.co.uk
Confidential advice for those dealing with the death of a close friend or family member.

DRINKWISE
www.drinkwise.co.uk
Advice on anything to do with alcohol.

EATING DISORDERS ASSOCIATION 0845 6347650
www.edauk.com
For those people suffering from an eating disorder, or their friends and family.

FRANK 0800 776600
www.talktofrank.com
For free and confidential advice about drugs and smoking (formerly the National Drugs Helpline).

GET CONNECTED 0808 8084994
www.getconnected.org.uk
For anyone who's run away or been thrown out of their home.

LGBT YOUTHLINE 0845 1130005
Support and advice for gay young people or those confused about their sexuality.

NATIONAL AIDS HELPLINE 0800 567123
For help and advice about AIDS or HIV.

NATIONAL MISSING PERSONS HELPLINE 0500 700700
www.missingpersons.org
Help for the families of missing persons.

RAPE CRISIS 0115 9003560
Support for rape sufferers.

RELATEEN 0845 4561310
For young people wanting to talk about family problems or relationships.